AMERICAN CAVEWALL SONNETS

AMERICAN CAVEWALL SONNETS

C. T. SALAZAR

BULL★CITY
PRESS
DURHAM, NORTH CAROLINA

American Cavewall Sonnets
Copyright ©2021 by C. T. Salazar.

Library of Congress Cataloging-in-Publication Data

Names: Salazar, C. T., 1992- author.
Title: American cavewall sonnets / C.T. Salazar.
Description: Durham, NC : Bull City Press, [2021].
Identifiers: LCCN 2020034757 | ISBN 9781949344202 (paperback) | ISBN 9781949344219 (ebook)
Subjects: LCGFT: Poetry.
Classification: LCC PR6119.A386 A44 2021 | DDC 821/.92--dc23
LC record available at https://lccn.loc.gov/2020034757

Published in the United States of America
Book design: Spock and Associates
Cover Art: Wildstyle Still Life by Collin van der Sluijs

Published by
BULL CITY PRESS
1217 Odyssey Drive
Durham, NC 27713
www.BullCityPress.com

TABLE OF CONTENTS

CAVEWALL SONNET

Wolf milk and wilderness   America.
Romulus and Remus built   a city
but it couldn't hide the animal in
their hearts: a river-child discovers blood
when he searches for a blessing. Hold your
motherland in your mouth, all marble and
doomed, a single lozenge of loss. Heaven
fell into the pond and killed all the fish.

Even in the shape of a boy I can
wear the morning. Daisies behind my ear.
Minutes thin, gold arm hairs. Blackberry vine
tied around my wrist. Look: under this field,
the only battle my father lost. Place
your ear right here   if you want to listen.

AMERICAN CAVEWALL SONNET

This is my box of twilight and inside
flickers everything   that disappeared when
we weren't looking, like glaciers and God,
the lonely astronaut waving as she
drifts from one starfield to another. Here's
the stone I found that glimmered in my hands
like a promise made mineral. My name
the frozen lake my body treads across.

This time, I'll walk into the house and ask
why my hands feel so dirty. A rose pinned
to my shirt like a throbbing ear, an ear
listening to the wreckage scraping at
the bottom of your words. The candle flame
like a tongue asking the room for water.

AMERICAN CAVEWALL SONNET

The fountain clogged with plague frogs and our hair
went unwashed. I said no, because you asked
if prayer worked. A hammer works. A man
is work to a mushroom no matter what
he's buried with—   I know none of this sounds
like an apology, but bear   with me:
the sunflower field was so dazzling
I missed the funeral (the truck wouldn't start).

Here's a country of statues crushed under
the weight of migrating ladybugs.   If
men could, they would melt other men down to
gold.   Mercy, you said, as if the fire
blew itself out. As if the town's missing
children woke up in the silo unharmed.

AMERICAN CAVEWALL SONNET

St. Peter's dried colon stuffed with honey-
suckle to mask the scent: the dove's direct
descendant perched in an ark-shaped cage, but
the relics of our fathers were never
so gentle. Boar tusk and ripped shirt. Buckshot
breath rising from the wound. I thought the fog
looked like wedding dresses falling over
the grass. Called them my sisters and followed.

In the dark, I was called beautiful but
I wasn't. Each step down the staircase broke
a promise: the lilies in my hand meant
it was June. My mother's rug still rolled up.
The room smelled like paint but we couldn't see—
We held our hands in front of us like this.

AMERICAN CAVEWALL SONNET

Dear oblivion   in the shape of a
human brain. Dear furnace of coal: how could
you? Could you, if I begged, make me look less
like the barbed wire was sharpened in my
likeness? Like the lily opening as
my mother's palm also   opens. This is
not to say her hands were fragile   no, I
remember the night she held a red flame

without flinching. Without saying, tell me
the shovel despises its work,   always
covering someone but never finding
the next step in mourning. Tell me this mask
looks nothing like my face, even if the
cosmos's big blue fingers pluck all our days.

AMERICAN CAVEWALL SONNET

The fires my father started O Lord.
Once, he found a sleeping bear and named him
Ramses. I am the bowl he cries in
at night, when the body is too simple
to break into meaningful music or
halve like fruit after a sharp knife. His jaw
where I look for the mountains gone. Under
his tongue the names of sleeping stars   wake.

For God so loved the world, he sobbed angels
and circus animals as it starved, and
He named these misplaced creatures *fathers.* My
father was always talking in his sleep.
Baby boy, the hurt I've brought others will
visit you soon, as a beggar limping.

AMERICAN CAVEWALL SONNET

This is the gospel of barking dogs. Saint
Augustine licking his paw. I never
talked about what I saw   in the river:
the believers who drowned. The blue pillars
of their bodies. My face painted the
same hour of daybreak. I promise   I
looked for you in the shattered mosaic
made from the salvaged chips of empire.

Darkness is a plate we pass,   terrible
taste we inherit. The church walls have cracked
from the heat that hatched and never flew out.
The kitchen where we dried our feet and wiped
rain out of our faces is painted and
has forgotten us: our thralling hours.

AMERICAN CAVEWALL SONNET

Hatchet Hatchet Hatchet Hatchet Hatchet
Hatchet Hatchet Hatchet (Hatchet) Hatchet
Hatchet Hatchet Hatchet Hatchet Hatchet
Hatchet Hatchet Hatchet Hatchet Hatchet
Hatchet Hatchet   -(a-che)-   Hatchet Hatchet
Hatchet Hatchet Hatchet Hatchet Hatchet
Hatchet Hatchet Hatchet Hatchet Hatchet
Hatchet (Hatch)

        et Hatchet Hatchet Hatchet

]   *Hope   Hope   Hope Hope Hope*
]   *Hope Hope Hope   Hope Hope*
]   *Hope   Hope Hope   Hope Hope*
]   *Hope   Hope   Hope Hope   Hope*
]   *Hope Hope Hope Hope Hope*
]   *Hope Hope Hope Hope Hope*

AMERICAN CAVEWALL SONNET

I tried to mouth hope but kept saying hatch
-et. Sing something to stay awake. Here's
a song about our ancestors: they wore
masks for fear of angels knowing their faces.
They fastened sails to their boats. Paradise,
mother says, hides   behind old family
photographs—the dark we hold but dare not
open. Empty bird nest in the old barn.

When I remember you   I remember
the animal we built out of stray bones
from the riverbed. The relic-rich ground:
the half-buried horseshoe I tripped over.
You shake sun from your hair—I'll wear your pearls.
All the trees of the field will clap their hands.

AMERICAN CAVEWALL SONNET

The rifle scope was a failure indeed
of the imagination—look through here
and everything becomes   a target.
When I feel like prey, I raise my hands and
look up. The train is covered in moss like
an animal too big to bury.   Tracks
in the tall grass lace the earth lovelessly.
What broke the horse more than our father's laugh?

Because the well was deeper than we knew,
the gun, falling, turned into many things:
a cloud of thunder. A phoneful of my
father's voice on the line—*Hello?* When you
fell, they told me, the piano groaned as
ants marched that sorrowful beast from the house.

AMERICAN CAVEWALL SONNET

In this version Perseus holds my head
and all the soldiers turn to piled feathers.
Now collapse. Summer-dried troop of boys gone
angelic soft. A brave boy called me a
beam of moonlight when his father wasn't
looking. I'm all babel of tongues for you:
bird of prey boy, bloom boy. I could love you
all. I could call you whatever you want.

Bring the knife and bring the choir. Bring the
song that goes *Breath of life, Lord, breach of law.*
I brought my hands and was told   Yes, that's all
you need   now hold this   careful not to point
at yourself   it's loaded   remember if
you pull the trigger you make new altars.

AMERICAN CAVEWALL SONNET

In the far corner of Yahweh's great mouth
-ful of greenery is where my mother
asked to lie down. The prayer she tied to
a sparrow's foot with her ribbon read *Yes*
we have sinned but we have several great
excuses.　　　　The underside of logic
is still the softest place to be barefoot.
I walked it once. I didn't want to leave.

The map to heaven I made on my palm
smeared when I held your hand. I wore my best
shirt. I dipped the cherries in chocolate.
Everything I burned / I burned for warmth,
even this layer of skin, soft as a
swan shaking against its own reflection.

AMERICAN CAVEWALL SONNET

What do I look like now, without warpaint
and dirt in my teeth? *Wer* means man: *war* means
God picked a flower and named it Abraham.
       God blew on a dandelion and
we went searching for a home. Wolves came and
insects came, and then insects left. Voices,
maybe mine, mourned the trees but the trees fell
anyway. And we had plenty of time.

[suffer not]   the sun getting heavier
by the moment [suffer not] my father's
handprint left in the sawdust [suffer not]
the things we touch that dare remember us
[summer not]   like a season caught in my
hair but my face slowly becoming his

AMERICAN CAVEWALL SONNET

I have written here an index of things
too beautiful to lose but we lost them
anyway: stained glass shepherds reaching out
for your hand with enough light to make it
believable. The tree whose bark was so
bright, children cut milk from its tender roots.
The shallow creek we never named but swore
we loved the reflection of our faces.

      what is control   what is another year
      without touch darling what will happen I
      don't know   I don't know   soon the oil will
      run out   we will burn   still America
      is just a word   it means   we couldn't mine
      answers   we had to dig into ourselves

AMERICAN CAVEWALL SONNET

The amount of muscle it takes to make
a mistake. Beware: the honeycomb is
pleasing. Symmetry wants you to feel just
as purposed, but I already put on
all these feathers. I already kissed all
the other lonely boys and they melted
like snow angels. Like a thin bone of light-
ning, we hardly last.   Still we break open.

Surrender. Sway. Say whatever you need
if it means the wheels of God don't crush you
into flakes of starlight and arrowhead.
It doesn't matter how favorable
your faith in our spin. It doesn't matter
how good your grip: the world is rudderless.

SONNET RIVER

Everything in the house will catch fire,
if you can believe that. Mississippi
burns you last if it loves you, and now all
your neighbors keep an axe in the house.
A dog on a chain means some angers you
can own but never trust, tricycle child.
The sound of a bell means someone wants you
to answer the door. Don't keep them waiting.

Baby I'll be your bullet-peppered stop
sign—our steady aim and your favorite
smear of stars to shoot at. Bounce a bullet
off a church bell. If the ringing reaches
God, he'll bless our names, call us his children
of King James and Remington: lightning bolt.

;;;

Of King James and Remington, lightning, bolt
action—all of these can fill the body
with new knowledge. In some gospels, God's grace
gets lost before it gets here, and hardens
from a river into a rattlesnake.
I press every cow skull to my chest
looking for that holy hum. I whistle
to dead birds but no miracle happens.

Every eulogy with the river
involved proves how hungry our river
grows each season. Season of broken neck.
Season of derailed train dangling from
the railroad bridge. And so says the river:
this is plenty. This is more than enough.

;;;

This is plenty—this is more than enough
field to follow your shadow into shape
-lessness. Surely it's a blessing to leave
the light and not feel lonely. You undress
me of my apologies and say I
look better without them. You know me best
beneath the dark river of stars, the spools
of barbed wire dragging across heaven.

After Adam was buried, Eve begged God
to let her keep some part of her husband,
so God dropped Adam's new heart in her hands.
She couldn't believe how heavy it was.
The children cried when they saw it gleaming—
in this telling, God called the heart *Axe head*.

;;;

In this telling, God called the heart *Axe head
cleaved deep in the body's bark*. My body
dark as the moon's inside. November's jaw
bridled to the cold. Crickets crushed under
horse hooves and my belief the next life
will need their little song for intervals
between falling toward softer light. Please keep
your hand in my hair as long as you want.

You in the field. You holding my father's
revolver, heavy as a handshake. What
war is waiting for us to lie down long
enough to forget our names? Every
bullet will be fired in due time. Love,
every belief grows teeth to chew you.

;;;

Every belief grows teeth to chew you
tenderly. If you ever feel swallowed,
take my hand. Dangle your feet from the fence
when you miss me and I'll shake all the dust
from the hymnals to name each floating god
-speck after our grandmothers. Don't forget
to water the plants. What's the heart if not
a teapot of blood carried in the chest?

You called me a piano turned over,
and you knew the setting sun was a man
walking toward me who needed firewood
more than he needed song. If the season
whittles us down, hallelujah our spines.
Praise our hollow bell bodies still ringing.

CAVEWALL SONNET

This room was no longer, so I put it
back together / I put it back in my
mind / I put it in the back of my mind.
I put the flowers in your favorite
vase, the one that breaks at the end of this
sentence. At the end of the world I'm told
a prayer could harden into a full
moon bright enough to guide our fathers back.

Even a whisper can bruise. *Little fish,*
whispered God, *what have you become?* The night
we wrapped ourselves in the curtains and danced
to Rhapsody In Blue, I never asked
why the men would turn to stone at the sight
of us. Even if black eye—love, touch me.

NOTES

"This is plenty. This is more than enough" is from Geoffrey Hill's "September Song."

"Sonnet River" is for Mississippi.

ACKNOWLEDGMENTS

Many thanks to the editors of the following publications, where some of these sonnets previously appeared, often in earlier forms:

EcoTheo Review

Foundry

The Rumpus

Tinderbox Poetry Journal

Gracious thanks to poet Beth Gordon, who read the earliest renditions of these sonnets. Gracious thanks to poets R. A. Villanueva and Ben Niespodziany, who read the manuscript in its earliest form.

ABOUT THE AUTHOR

C. T. Salazar is a Latinx poet and librarian from Mississippi. His debut collection, *Headless John the Baptist Hitchhiking*, is forthcoming in 2022 from Acre Books. He's the author of two other chapbooks: *This Might Have Meant Fire* (Bull City Press) and *Forty Stitches Sewing a Body Against a Ramshackle Night* (Animal Heart Press). He's the 2020 recipient of the Mississippi Institute of Arts and Letters award in poetry. His poems have appeared in *The Cincinnati Review, The Rumpus, Beloit Poetry Journal, 32 Poems, RHINO,* and elsewhere.

ALSO BY C. T. SALAZAR

This Might Have Meant Fire

Forty Stitches Sewing a Body Against a Ramshackle Night

Headless John the Baptist Hitchhiking